The Itinerant Girl's Guide to Self-Hypnosis

lyrical prose by

Joanna Penn Cooper

Brooklyn Arts Press · New York

The Itinerant Girl's Guide to Self-Hypnosis
© 2014 Joanna Penn Cooper

ISBN-13: 978-1-936767-30-4

Cover art "Oileáin Bhríde I" by Simone Kearney.
Book design by Joe Pan.

All rights reserved. No part of this publication may be reproduced by any means existing or to be developed in the future without the written consent by the publisher.

Published in the United States of America by:
Brooklyn Arts Press
154 N 9th St #1
Brooklyn, NY 11249
www.BrooklynArtsPress.com
info@brooklynartspress.com

Library of Congress Cataloging-in-Publication Data

Cooper, Joanna, 1971-
 [Poems. Selections]
The Itinerant Girl's Guide to Self-Hypnosis / [Lyrical Prose] by Joanna Penn Cooper. -- First edition.
     pages cm
"Lyrical Fiction."
"Distributed to the trade by Small Press Distribution / SPD"--T.p. verso.
 ISBN 978-1-936767-30-4 (pbk. : alk. paper)
 I. Title.

PS3603.O58265A6 2014
811'.6--dc23
                          2013048938

10 9 8 7 6 5 4 3 2 1
FIRST EDITION

Acknowledgements

This book is for my mother, Karol, and my grandmother, Marion.

Grateful acknowledgement is made to the editors of the following publications, in which portions of this manuscript first appeared: *Best American Poetry* blog, *Boog City, Dicey Brown, Everyday Genius, Lyre Lyre, Muse, Opium, Pindeldyboz, Scapegoat Review, South Dakota Review, Supermachine,* and *Tygerburning Literary Journal.*

Several of these works also appeared in the chapbook *Mesmer,* from dancing girl press.

The piece that begins with the line "Tips for the Conservation and Renewal of Vital Energies" is after a work by Ron Padgett. "I think it's time we stop, / Children, what's that sound? / Everybody look what's goin' down." and "You don't have to say you love me, / just be close at hand." are lyrics from Buffalo Springfield and Dusty Springfield, respectively. Special thanks to Todd Colby for an appropriated and modified line: "I will always have the sense that leaving is easy, until I get to the next place and get my hair cut for company." The line "Most things happen at dusk" is adapted from a line by Jack Spicer from the poem "Imaginary Elegies." (Spicer's line is "Most things happen in twilight.") The lines "The dream where the sleeper is lying prostrate / turns transparent" by Tranströmer comes from his poem "The Man Who Awoke with Singing over the Roofs." The following sentence is from a piece by Kate Lutzner: "I consulted the farmer's almanac about whether I should get my hair cut, and when I did get it cut, I looked like a boy." The words from Cornel West are from the documentary *Examined Life.* The line "To die is different from what any one supposed, and luckier" comes from Walt Whitman's "Song of Myself."

My thanks to Paula McLain, Malena Mörling, and Joan Larkin for their mentorship, encouragement, and warmth. Thank you to all the faculty and to my cohort in New England College's MFA program for their help and support along the way. For their kind and incisive readings of my work; for inspiring me with their own creativity; and for their friendship, thanks to J. Hope Stein, Todd Colby, Annmarie O'Connell, Lauren Gordon, Douglas Piccinnini, Kate Lutzner, Amanda Emerson, and to my brother, Alex Lenhoff. Thanks to Mihaela Moscaliuc for a thorough and helpful reading of an earlier version of this manuscript and to Brooklyn Arts Press editor Joe Pan for all the work he put into the book. Thank you Shanna Compton for talking genre with me. I am grateful for the time I got for writing and revision at Vermont Studio Center, and thank you to everyone who supported me on my way there and while there. Thank you—so much—to my family. Thank you, Clifton. Thank you, Elias.

The Itinerant Girl's Guide to Self-Hypnosis

Nothing much happened today, unless you count seeing a hawk on a low branch in Central Park. Unless you count going to the Guggenheim and getting dizzy.

Haunted tries to happen, but I'm too dizzy to notice.

Strong iced coffee. Meeting a friend for lunch, I talk in a very animated way for thirty minutes before the coffee personality goes away again.

Summer birthday. Wildflowers, Hudson.
Thirty-nine and _____

Few summer activities to report in July. I travel down Manhattan to sit in the Quiet Reading Room. I'm looking into Bernadette Mayer. A man follows me into the Quiet Reading Room and sits on the other couch. I make a face at him. I start reading Bernadette Mayer and making little snorts and chortles. The man gets up and leaves.

When we were children, we were all sort of dry and made of hair and limbs, with boys just a bit warmer and drier. Then we were teenagers and made of shoulders and hips and different hair.

Voice says, *The hum and click braiding.* Voice says, *tethered in the paddock.* (What's a paddock?)

I call my grandmother and she says, *Don't ever allow yourself to get used to something that's not good for you.* Useful all-purpose advice.

For a few days, I skulk around the apartment thinking phrases like, *It liked to have killed him.* Some of my family might say such a thing.

Found in summer notebook: *Stop having ideas about ideas.* (Tethered in a paddock.)

Yeats said it this way: *Tragic joy.*

Woke up thinking of motherhood because I have not done that. In high school I saved my brother from choking on a Cheerio in his high chair, so maybe he'll take care of me when I'm old, even though he doesn't remember. I'm pretty sure I turned him upside down and everything, until his face wasn't red anymore, and then he just went on with his day.

Woke up thinking with affection of my student who takes my same bus, who said in class (gently, firmly), "That flip-flopping. That's how we learn."

Cornel West says we can stop worrying about "Wholeness" in the Romantic sense. Twain knew. West says we all got here through the "funk of life." "The love push that got us here," he says. It's easier to imagine if your mother was a hippie, which mine was sort of, and young.

And what if that funky vessel turns around and buys you flannel pajamas with monkeys for Christmas, and noise-reducing headphones, and reads all your poems, even though she doesn't like poems? If I never bring more people here, how do I pay it back? How does the love push work then?

Voice says, "Be your own funky vessel." The good-enough funk.

Have you ever teared up at brunch when you were supposed to be deciding what to order?

Was it due to all the uncertainty of life, the way things keep *changing*? How nothing is fixed?

Did you enjoy your mimosa anyway? The caramelized apples? Were the caramelized apples a blessing, even though the man to your left kept talking about renting a hotel room to learn all the three-letter Scrabble words?

Afterward, did you sit in the park and watch a little girl with straight posture and a braid do a dainty run back and forth to fetch large rocks and hurl them with force upon the flagstones? Like this: *run run*, hands out at sides, *run run*, THROW the rock down to see if it breaks?

Did she at one point come back with a walk that involved lifting her feet high, as if stepping through fairy dew at a ballet recital? *Step. Step. Step.* THROW the rock down.

To die is different from what any one supposed, and luckier. Have you had this line in your head for a while? Is living like that, also? Luckier but more painful?

Suppose we embrace it? The dream-like rhetorical bent. The rocks and the stepping through dew. What then?

How might it be, she used to wonder, to be an other girl? Someone whose name starts with K. Someone whose skin is milk and mauve, someone who's tall, even taller. With secret talents and an other laugh, an other sadness, a secret grief-life all her own.

Having always been this nervous scapula, knife-sharp eyes. Having never fully betrayed the music of the spheres. Having never let it move through her. Having found some salt of her salt on the lips of two to four others. Having held in her chest a delicate paper folding fan from a 1920s tourist town. Having tried. Having tried. Having been one with the birds. Having held her sleeping brother sideways when he was four, forgetting his age, his legs dangling like that. Having been held by others. Having observed and having been observed. The family mouth. The family heart in the family throat. The *go look at the moon*. Box hedges. Swimming pools. Elementary school smell of heated paint and dust. Having learned the stories. Having failed to learn them enough. The steel-toed boots. The frying pan. The great-great-uncle dead in Mexico. The great-great-uncle dead in the quarry. Plumbing the ancestral line. Plumbing the astral one. Alone with one's books. Alone with one's own green heart.

I was born in a town of vegetable gardens, anthropology professors, pregnant teenagers drinking Cokes, and signs in bar windows saying, *No Indians*. A place of myth and history. Kansas. This morning I woke thinking, *I have all of it left to do*, and wondering what it was. My best artist friend has a five-year plan that reads something like, *Build a mountain of plywood. Learn to breathe out of my eyelids. Love.* I guess I'll do that, too. Some version of that. I guess I'll learn to pray without ceasing by committing to my part. Here's what I found recently: A worksheet from 3rd or 4th grade divided into two halves asking, *What makes you happy?* and *What makes you sad?* For sad, I drew a dog getting hit by a car and a horse with a broken leg. Sad for the animals. For happy, I was there in crayon with puffy pigtails, enjoying an ice cream cone on a sunny day. With tulips. There was also a drawing of a shirtless guy surfing an extravagant pompadour of a wave, a moon man in profile above, having a laugh in a cage of pointy stars. I wrote a caption: *At night*. I may have been born chronically homesick. But don't tell me I don't know happy.

You're in my Hall of Fame room holding a ginger seal pup with a fabulous mullet. You have the mullet, not the seal pup. I'm in your Hall of Fame room going all post-apocalyptic child star, killing and roasting my own venison while wearing glorious deerskin gaiters. If I had news about my plasma, you'd be the person I'd write to, to take my mind off the news about my plasma. If you needed someone to hold the sides of your head to keep your mind ok, I'd totally write you a poem that metaphorically held the sides of your head. In our previous friendship, back in time, we were some of those proto-human toddlers who took painting lessons in a cave ritual about painting lessons. As a middle-aged man of fifteen, you invented dung sculpture, blowing everyone's mind. I had my own project, blowing on fiery twigs to create shapes like those little brass angels that fly by the heat of candle flame at Christmas. But nothing like that at all.

Subway report, 10:55 PM. *Who will I be if I let go the steering wheel?* is what I'm thinking as I cross the Manhattan Bridge by subway. To my left, a guy named James has taken out his phone, is leaving an elaborate message involving his name, address, and a long string of numbers. To my right a group of teenage boys needs a haircut. They are young. They are puppies. One is talking about the finals they have yet to take—*History, Spanish, English*—while he feels the face of the friend next to him, squeezing his cheeks and mouth into strange positions. The friend whose face is being squeezed is impassive, stares straight ahead. The boys fall silent, hands to themselves. A man with an upright bass across the aisle lifts his eyes to meet mine. We're back in the tunnel. I experiment with leaving my hands off the wheel. I think, *Hello, lamb.*

The way Nietzsche says we limit the poor squirrel by calling it "squirrel." (Does Nietzsche say that?) The way your roommate said he sometimes glances at a squirrel, and then *becomes* it for a second. I did this sitting on your couch, drawing a cartoon map—you were drawing—and in your bed. You were my transitional object—my fort-da? Or we were both the boat and the shiny thing we'd spotted bobbing in the distance. Both of us were both these things. It's like me and the tired lady getting on the bus—how I will suddenly *be* her, and, just for a moment, love her.

It's funny to think of your own grandmother as a skinny little kid with dirty feet and braids standing under a tree in Spencer, North Carolina and telling some other little 1930s kids, "You may not know this, but I am part Indian. Indeed, my people came from the coast of Virginia, where there are many blue-eyed Indians." And then later going to the movies all day by herself for fifteen cents during the war and running home late, zigzagging through alleys so that no one could follow her in the dark, her feet smacking the cooling pavement as she mutters to herself, "That's what they want you to think. Well, I think for myself, thank you very much. You can't pull the wool over these eyes. There are all sorts of people in this world, and no two alike. That's a fact." Running, running toward home, her older brothers asleep in ditches in France.

All the sadnesses of childhood. Being pigeon-toed and loved, dirty blond and loved. The nervous tapping, the counting of steps. Free lunch tokens at school. But listen—I was once in a dance recital. It may have been over in a blur. I may have forgotten my steps or stumbled through them. But even now I love the costume and how someone paid to rent it for me. There is a photograph of a child in a showgirl outfit. Hair up. Ringlets. Green and white striped satin bodice. Fringe. Fishnets.

My grandmother says: One night John came home from one of his trips and told me to look at the dogwoods blooming in the yard. Came up the stairs and woke me up to say, *Look out the window. The trees are giant snowballs.* So white, he said, they seemed to shine.

My grandmother says this house reminds her of a dying flower. The petals just lie where they fall.

She says: There used to be a great, huge house on that corner when I was a child. Two old sisters who wore long black dresses and button shoes lived there. And one of the sisters used to climb up into the magnolia tree and look down at everyone walking by. I guess she was about eighty. Same age I am now.

Says: I could climb that tree if I wanted to.

By the time I knew him, he was tired from the cancer, but he would take out his teeth to make me laugh. I used to point at his tattoo of a cartoon dog in a sailor hat, and he would say, "I got that in the war."

He died the night before Easter. I didn't know what that meant.

My uncle John tells this story: "Well, I guess Dad would have a little too much to drink, and he would take the straight ladder out back and hold it straight up in the air and try to climb it before it fell. One day I watched him do that over and over. I think he really thought he could do it. But I guess if anyone could have done it, it would have been Dad."

"We are all fish swimming along, not even realizing we're in water," my grandfather used to say.

One time I bought this postcard that I never sent to anyone—a black and white photograph of a ladder propped against storefront letters that spelled "faith."

At Easter time I travel to MoMA and speak to a guard about how to avoid other people.

I become friends with a girl in a stroller on the subway by making hello beak fingers at her and squinting, even as her best friend remains the used paint stirrer she holds for luck.

I shuffle. I whine. I regard the daffodils in Central Park and feel that they regard me back.

I enter the Natural History Museum when everyone else is pushing out, then leave my guests at the sign for bioluminescence to go meditate upon the stolen Tlingit spoons.

I greet the lilies.

I mark, and I am marked.

On the brick wall opposite my window, light and leaf shadow. Graffiti reading *Joey 79*. Inside, light on the lap of the chair.

My grandmother on the phone telling me what her mother used to say. *Anybody that's in the same mood all the time is crazy.* The words come to me across space and across time. Then, *You have to travel on the road a long time and learn lots of things.*

At the cafe, a silver fork engraved with a cursive *H. A.*

Out the window, a white-blond pigeon walking by, face colored like a hawk, followed by a fat wolf-dog on a leash, affable as a talking bear.

A squirrel chasing a sparrow.

Light and air and leaves moving. Even water and a stone wall. A cheese sandwich. Espresso.

At the park, a remote control bird is stuck in the tallest tree, twittering. The girl puts her helmet back on and runs her bike up the hill. A boy speeds by on a tiny motorcycle singing. *HEEEY HEEEEY. Boom. Boom. Boom. Boom-de-boom.*

Two teenaged girls walk up the hill, holding and swinging hands. They bump hips, drop hands, stop to talk, continue on. Both have wavy brown hair past their shoulders, and the one with bigger hips holds her chin lifted, as if her face is helping her climb.

Later, looking up to see the moon, but it is only light from the window opposite.

It's true, I could be a lyrical child, kneeling under the dogwoods in dappled light and breeze to channel messages, when the air spoke in murmurs like dreaming. Other times, I wasn't that. I lied about small things, stole candy, pretended to sleepwalk, threw a plate of spaghetti at the side of the house. I had a manual typewriter and used it for yellow journalism and blaming notes to my mother. I made up stories after lunch to spook the kids at school, working at their minds until a chink opened. I did strange magic at slumber parties, getting everyone half-hypnotized and muted to the spot. *Light as a feather, stiff as a board.*

I dreamed the moon was the hugest it had ever been, which helped explain our behavior. The real things, though, were the hawk on a near tree when we woke yesterday, and, last night, wind like wind from *Close Encounters*, shaking our front door five flights up. All these shifts in weather and bird, all this feeling of winter being rent—by which I mean *tearing, torn*, but I guess there's that other kind of rent, too. Did you ever read *Howards End*? For Forster, you go on trusting at the risk of being robbed. Whatever you lose is "rent to the ideal." This is all a workshop I'm paying for. The rent is slush and chill and knowing we will die, which is also part of the workshop. The cost of the class is the subject of the class, a seminar called "Difficult and Wondrous: The Costs and Rewards of Walking on Through." Syllabus forthcoming.

I will always have the sense that leaving is easy, until I get to the next place and get my hair cut for company. Nightmares about having to leave, for me, are also nightmares about having to stay. Like that kid that time (my brother), I'm apt to start screaming if I can't get on a transatlantic flight with my hobo bundle. So I'll retire to the bushes by the front stoop to eat carrots, sing mournful songs, and look for my runaway turtle, as we all did as children. It's hard to grow up in poems when you've been working on the same project all these years. I'll be here in my closet office with a bowl of popcorn and a bare bulb to keep me warm. Besides, no one wants to hear about adult heaviness. Not the wind. Not even the road.

I remember that in Knoxville some people had pictures of Jesus in their houses, or talked about Jesus a lot or about whether certain things were sins. Maybe they were Baptists. We never talked about Jesus. We were Lutherans, except really we were nothing because we never went to church. I was only Lutheran when I stayed with my grandmother. Even then, she and I would go to Lutheran church one weekend and Catholic church the next because she was thinking things over.

One Baptist lady, some kid's mother, asked me on the stairs if I was a woman yet. I said, "Uh, no. I'm only ten." Then the kid whispered, "She means did you get your period yet." And I said, "I'm only ten." The woman gave me a smug smile and told me that her daughter—a strangely polite girl with short curly brown hair—was *already a woman*. I felt bad for the girl for that and for having that mother. I felt bad for Jesus, looking out over our heads as we stood there on the stairs in a duplex down the road from my apartment building.

When I was a teenager, I knew a thing or two. I stayed in my room being skinny and having bangs, listening to Bauhaus and lifting 3 lb weights. I drew pretty good portraits of my own face. I learned to drive stick, and I would drive farther out into the suburbs to go to the mall and walk around drinking Dr. Pepper and chewing candy and being mildly disgusted with all the people, who seemed to be sinking of their own accord. On the way there I'd look for the Eagles on the radio, in order to demonstrate that the Eagles are always on the radio, and to further demonstrate that—for good or bad—my vocal range exactly matched that of one Don Henley. On the way back, I would listen to Heart or Fleetwood Mac, which reminded me of my childhood in the '70s, a time of honest belting and bad vibes. Boys at school would talk to me in class, and I guess I would just look at them or say something weird about *The Sorrows of Young Werther* or something, because after a while they'd get nervous and blurt out, "I guess that's how people dress in *Europe*." Then we'd both turn around, and class would start.

I'm running into the diner to pluck $20 from his ceremoniously outstretched hand and running back out to pay the cabbie. I am a little late and showing up without my wallet, some part of me, I guess, wanting to cement some idea he might have of me after all these years. Flying by the seat of my pants! Ker-flustered! Then I'm back inside and he is hugging me harder than I expected, one of my arms accidentally curled inside the hug, my fist at my shoulder, so that I seem to be protecting myself. We are looking at each other and talking talking and glancing at our menus, looking and talking. How good to see ourselves! Then the waitress comes, and I panic and order French toast. With strawberries! My French toast arrives and I'm learning again: French toast is good; life is not an emergency; no matter how many years go by, every time we see each other for the rest of our lives—how many times? a handful?—a moderately heavy string will be stretched from my solar plexus to his, and this string will make us glad and bemused and slightly uncomfortable. I'm offering him French toast and he's taking strawberries.

I am nine. I am sitting on a brown couch at 10 AM. I'm wearing tube socks and a rayon nightgown with the lace trim half torn off by my foot. Or I'm wearing my Bob Dylan t-shirt nightgown that Paul brought me last time. I like how Bob Dylan's hair sticks out all around. It's spring. My mother is sleeping. She hung crystals in the windows, and this is the time of day when the sun hits the crystals and sends bits of light onto the wood floor and the dust. We don't live in the house anymore. We live in an apartment. We don't have cats and a dog anymore, but we have plants. I bring my knees up to my chest and pull the nightgown over them and from that position look through a book of circus freaks. I study Jo-Jo the Dog-Faced Boy and feel a tugging kinship.

I'm not lonely. I don't think about TV. I don't think about when my mother will wake up. When Lisa comes to the door, I tell her I can't play. She gets really mad, almost as mad as a person can get. She tells me she hopes I rot in there and stomps down the stairs. I close the door and make a glass of Strawberry Quik. I sit on the floor with my glass. I study the bits of light and the floating bits of dust.

What drew me in was the jaunty good humor with which she approached every little thing in the fourth grade, even being late for school. There was the time she told the sour-faced teacher that homework "cramped her style," even rumors that she had undressed for almost every boy in class, taking them across the street after school to her house on the corner when no one was home. I couldn't get enough. But when I was invited in to her house on Flenniken Avenue it was dark and musty inside, with the grandparents' pill bottles piled on the kitchen table. There were too many collectible dolls under the bed and lining the walls of the room she shared with her mother. In the little-used front room, we were to be quiet and gentle in our movements. To the old people, even children should act like old people. There we huddled between the bench and the piano, Angela whispering her story about the Donny and Marie dolls. It wasn't sordid, their affair. What they had was a star-crossed love. Out on the back porch, the glee she barely contained during her days at school spilled out, as she twirled and stomped, showing me her clogging lessons, droll about the eyes and mouth and hair.

It was her mother who first noticed it, how when the girl was eighteen, men's gazes would sometimes linger on her for a moment, curious. At times, the daughter's own gaze rested half a step inside herself, her eyes down and to the right, like those Pre-Raphaelite women. Twice, people had commented on this. "You look like one of those Pre-Raphaelite paintings," they said. That isn't how she saw herself, though. And she bristled at references to young women "blooming." "I'm not a flower," she would say. Mostly she stayed in her room and read books. Boys at the dorm would come by to watch TV and propose massages.

She wasn't a Catholic, but she began to think of convents—silence, the low swoosh of robes, the feeling of beads moving through her fingers, the smooth wood in the chapel, and other women gliding by, their gazes also resting on God Within. Mostly she thought of the silence and how she would step into the courtyard alone with the green and the arches, the statues and the low, protecting sky.

In the Smoky Mountains it is pleasant to stumble if someone with oversized hands catches you in his hands like baseball mitts.

This is called dating.

We had come to see the intersection of fixed objects with the changing fields around them. In the pictures, I'm a little pale and histamined, bleary in the face, and winter is coming, but we got the second-to-last bus out before spring and it was the best thing we ever did today. On the bus back, the couples leaned their heads on each other in different ways, and C's shoulder was bony, but I put my hat there and leaned. Still bony. Soon my head was somewhere between his stomach and lap, and I drowsed for twenty minutes, holding his hand, my head pressed hard into his abdomen. I felt the flesh under there—all that skin and sinew of a person who let me do these things to him now. After my nap I sat up and whispered fast, *I'm going to bite your face*, but I didn't. I think no one heard. I thought, *I could write that down*. Or I just thought, *I have someone I could bite their face*; then, *I have someone whose face I could bite*, all in that voice in my head that means I might write it down.

Dream of D:

Buries words in his backyard, 2-3 feet tall, made of some kind of foam. Primary colors. Reverse archaeology. He is energetic, preparing for a party. Everyone will wonder what words they're walking on. It will be stylish and arbitrary. Unnatural but organic.

Dream of J:

By the road at dusk. There is a tree with a spirit. We have to hurry and take pictures of the great indentation in the earth before it gets too dark. It is too dim, too beautiful. He is resting in the hole. I am learning to use my camera.

Dream of C:

Coming into the room, his t-shirt wet with blood. Wanting a reaction. Suddenly not kind, not safe. It is a project. Blooming flower of blood. I have no way of leaving and must continue reacting.

Dream of J (2):

He won't acknowledge that we're in the same village. We walk along the path of tall trees separately, each a little amused, a little irritated. But then at the old stone house, resting on the white bed. Breeze in the sheer drapes. He comments on the numinous atmosphere. *I taught him that word.*

We are standing at the far side of the whale tank at the aquarium when he says, "You do remind me of Alice." Certainly it happened—how waking life slips toward dream life sometimes, tips and dims and meets at the edges, the whales just under there, waiting to be fed. The press of families fades into background music, a tinkling toy piano playing a theme, aquarium stars like bits of crystal turning in their spheres.

He started out 5'8", but by the time their romance was over, he was 4'3", and she didn't know what to do with him. Sometimes he would sneak into her pocket when she was on her way out to the library and wait until she was in the middle of trying to remember something important before popping out under her armpit and humming love songs toward her ear. His hum was the hum of a forgetful mime. Overall, his personality was that of a juggler irritated by a parking ticket. Sometimes, though, he reminded her of a man with sad eyes, given to slicking down his hair with something that smelled like her grandfather, making her like him terribly. "Bright Eyes," her friends called him behind his back. And it was true: he was as impudent as Charlton Heston. Bounced on the balls of his feet when he walked.

He had taken up smoking to get back at his parents for giving him an alliterative name, but then one day he told her, "You don't know what sad is until you've seen the mattress your parents slept on your whole life thrown into a garbage truck." By then he had given up smoking, and she was about to move to Canada for reasons of her own, having to do with a movie she had once seen.

When she got there, she realized that he probably missed her, but that he was probably the kind of person who would allow himself one day to be sad before distracting himself with ukulele lessons. She occupied herself with arranging her spices and cheering up the dog, and then on the 17th day after she moved, she became very sad while measuring the coffee.

Because when someone else and I knew we would break up but had not yet done it, he took me to Lake Superior, Madeline Island, and we road our bikes down dark roads, crisp summer, blue sky, huge evergreens. This time he rode behind and beside me slowly, taking pictures.

Now think of a living deer, a young male in Wisconsin, who watches someone on a bike, looking put-out. Watch as it takes sudden confused steps toward us from the woods before stopping short as we sail on by.

I consulted the farmer's almanac about whether I should get my hair cut, and when I did get it cut, I looked like a boy. So then I consulted the I-Ching about whether to buy some makeup, and when I went to the store, the woman told me she wanted to try some products on me. She put me on a high stool, and I could feel her body's heat and magnetism as she leaned in to apply the eyeshadow. She told me that my eyes were very striking, like a bird's. Like an eagle's! I kind of liked it, but I kind of thought it was presumptuous.

After my makeover, I bought a short blue dress. It was so short it looked like a shirt. Maybe it was a shirt. Then I drove to my ex-boyfriend's house, and he said I looked good. He seemed a little dazed. He was barbecuing on the back porch, and I leaned over the railing and listened to the trees. After we had sex, I went home and consulted my Tarot cards. They said I shouldn't have done that. That I was a woman bound by ropes and surrounded by swords, afraid to make any move of her own. Afraid of the boat, afraid of the water, afraid of the shore.

Is a crumpet a popover? Is a loon a heron? I look up "loon" on my phone and feel troubled. A loon is so obviously not a heron.

I swear a great white heron once followed me around St. Paul for a week.

It looked like a prehistoric thing, but with white feathers, the way its feet hung down like that. Appeared with the spring and the decision to move again floating over me. That pull. And there it was, floating past the classroom window, so that I stopped in the middle of teaching and shouted, looking, I imagine, somewhat hypnotized.

And then later that same day it appeared over my car as I drove home. Then again as I sat in my chair reading—this great huge kite with side-headed eyes, gliding right between my brick building and the next, its eyes level with my eyes.

Who can you tell this to in New York? No one.

Dear Upstairs Neighbors,

There seems to be someone with a heavy tread who walks back and forth with shoes on, purposefully, in the mornings and in the evenings. Unfortunately, given the thin floors, we can hear this. It sounds very loud to us. We wish it weren't so.

When this building was first erected, it was envisioned *as an uptown utopia where middle class New Yorkers could live amidst a resort-like atmosphere.* In fact, *a 1924 advertisement published in the* New York Times *promised a doctor, dentist, valet, barber, beauty salon and taxi stand all on premises.* There was to be a bus to drive residents up the hill from the subway stop. The courtyard must have been lovely then, the fountain in working order, the plot of dirt around it planted with roses and vines. Now, as we know, the walkways are crumbling and certain areas have recently been marked off with yellow caution tape. Men from the former Yugoslavia call out to each other in the mornings as they fill in the courtyard cracks with cement. When I go down to do laundry in the afternoon, they are all taking a break on the stoop, not eating, not smoking, just lounging on the stairs and talking, and they give me a half-smirking, half-friendly smile and don't quite meet my eyes when I say hello.

[I don't know about you, but living in the city sometimes makes me feel like a clown, sort of like Giulietta Masina in Fellini's *Nights of Cabiria*, but less scrappy, bobby-socked Roman hooker and more tired-out, underemployed humanities PhD. I imagine, though (as happened to Cabiria), that the more pious, the more jaded, and the more wealthy city dwellers are looking at me and wondering about my funny walk, my ineffectual defenses, my strange combination of pertness and defeat, the vulnerability I can't hide from anyone.]

Do you think the floors of this building were always so thin? Did you hear the fight I had with my boyfriend last week about how offended I was that he hid the Newman-O's cookies from me because I tend to eat most of them before he gets to them? Have you ever seen a ghost in here? The other night, I woke up at around 3 AM to a sickly toxic smell of radiator paint—it was the first night the radiators had come on this fall—and for a moment I thought a young woman with straight dark brown hair was sitting cross-legged by my bed. Do people still say "Indian-style"? Then my eyes adjusted, and it was nothing, just a large mirror I have propped against the wall. It isn't that I saw myself in the mirror, just that suddenly the woman was gone, and the mirror was in her place. She was more of a girl really, but I tend to use the word "woman" for anyone above the age of 17, mostly due to my distaste for the way the word girl has been misapplied to women for so long. Was she a ghost girl or a dream or a trick of the eyes? I don't expect you to know, dear neighbor. But please ask your friend wearing soccer cleats to take them off and to find a new location in which to train miniature llamas to jump through hoops. Feel free to play your violin anytime, though. Perhaps the girl will like that.

Sincerely yours,
Downstairs

You may be just the tiniest bit agoraphobic on certain days, but if you've been sitting for several hours staring at your CV and your unpublished book manuscript, I recommend that you take a shower. You may then want to sit on the edge of the bed and stare into space for a few minutes before putting on some comfortable corduroys and the running shoes you bought for walking because, you know, maybe you'll take up running. (Probably not.) When you're ready to leave the house, impulsively pick up five poems and read them out loud in what you're thinking of as your "new reading voice." When you finally leave the house, realize that it's almost dinner time and decide to go to a restaurant for a salad and a $5 glass of wine when you realize it's happy hour and glasses of wine are only $5. Whether you want to or not, eavesdrop on the couple opposite you who seem to be on a first date. Their conversation will be painful to overhear. He will be doing all the talking, trying to very clearly indicate to her that he finds her attractive. She will be sitting very still, wearing her coat, and trying to decide how she feels about it all. Can this possibly end well? Pay your check, get up, and walk to the park. Walk briskly around for thirty minutes, pumping your arms a little. It will be two days after the vernal equinox, with deceptive sunshine, so that when you've gone once around the path, you are a little sweaty under your coat, but your gloveless hands will be red and freezing. Listen to the sound of aluminum bats striking baseballs. Accidentally do a weird little hop without breaking your stride when someone's half boxer, half pit bull lunges at you a little. When you come around to the baseball diamond a second time, it will be getting just the slightest bit dark and the field will be suddenly, uncannily empty. Everyone will have packed up and left just that quickly.

It is overcast and chilly in our invented city. It is Christmas, and we wear our sad faces over our calm faces. We sit inside ourselves, like we do. You have been a visitor here for twenty years, staying for longer and shorter visits, reading *People* in the corner on leather furniture, feeling blank and comforted. This is the place where someone makes you a sandwich, cutting up the small amount of onion into very small pieces because you asked, where someone calls out to you in a little voice, "Mini, where's my white blankie with the white fringe?" and you bring her the white blankie with the white fringe because, after all, she gave you life. You can say, "Hey! You're the portal through which I entered this world!" And she'll just look at you, eyes level, do a slight nod and say, "I know."

Just broke the globe paperweight thingy that served to stand papers up so you can see them when you are working on the computer. It had a little fish in it, swimming in the ocean. Who knew that the fish was actually swimming in an oily substance that is now all over my shirt and probably giving me some weird chemicals.

–Mom

Poor big-headed Marilyn Monroe in *The Misfits*, with her Tweety Bird forehead, is bothering my friend Amanda, who mimics her breathy neediness and snorts. Marilyn's character is saying she misses her *mother*. Isn't it funny, she says, I miss my mother. And the actor listening seems to believe that she does. And aren't we all, really, just sad, sedated, bosomy blondes— part canny Method, part broken baby? Or Montgomery Clift! Aren't all of us odd and handsome lisping cowboys, bandages about our heads?

Before I have to put my cat to sleep, I dream that I wheel him outside for some sun. He is a teenage boy with a degenerative disease, and his stomach is hurting, so I rub it for him. But we are enjoying the day, the sun and the grass and how we belong to each other but are separate, too. Tom Waits comes into the yard to do some landscaping. He is wearing his hat and suspenders, his undershirt and old suit pants. I say, "Hello, Tom Waits." Then Andy says, "Hello, Tom Waits." His voice comes out in a slightly strangled way because he is a boy with a degenerative disease, and also a cat. He is making a joke about how he can talk now and about how funny it all is. Then we laugh, and I'm thinking about how funny Andy has always been. We sit in the sun like ambassadors, like kids at a Kool-Aid stand.

Several nights now, you have been in one of a row of chairs on the shore line, not even realizing that you're washing around in the tide until the TV gets pulled away or the washing machine or the toddler whose hand you were holding. A kind of lullaby. The feeling when you were small, say seven, when you lay in bed, not wanting to sleep, not wanting to be alone, but resigned then. Holding a plastic thrift store toy, a white bulbous bird with light color airbrushed on the cheeks and wings. The hard plastic in your hands, the round shape of it, the old string coming out, a ring at the end: this was the kind of thing that could keep you company when you were smaller, but now you are just here alone with this toy cupped near your ear, playing it over and over, your mother perhaps listening from the other room, wondering. Alone in your sea canoe, the sea is darkness, glimmers of moon and darkest clouds. The lullaby doesn't anchor you anymore— it sends you back to your own devices. Cuts you free. The loneliness then, knowing that no one will fill this space for the rest of your life. Not really. And the aloneness is delicious, being adrift, clutching some other baby's Salvation Army toy.

Morning in firmly mid-May, and I'm out of bed and slouched in a chair with the left back quadrant of my head positioned toward the window, my left ear ready—as always—to catch the busy talking of the bird congeries. (*Congeries* is a word, but the word I'm thinking of would mean something between congeries and congress.) C's twitching waking twitched me awake this morning, and then he was washing every dish and making coffee. I lurch-toddled to the bathroom and peed vitamins, then lay down again. When I could, I rose and changed my t-shirt (why?), then sat on the bed and picked up the book that was there. I read these lines by Tranströmer: "The dream where the sleeper is lying prostrate / turns transparent." Unless he's making it up, Tranströmer has had the really mysterious fading into time of Swedish villages and orange light to ponder over. He's one of those strangers moving through time alone accompanied by wisps of dreams and scenery and sometimes other people. You might think, "Oh, I guess this lady is a stranger moving through time alone accompanied by light and mystery and other people. But where is her scenery? Why is her back to the window?" I can tell you this: it's still before noon. My morning dreams have turned transparent. It's bright out there, but something turned and faded in this room just now. The congeries is calming down, breaking into committees.

Tips for the Conservation and Renewal of Vital Energies

1. Don't worry about the dream where you bought a new pair of suede boots and they got ruined the same day. You never actually bought the boots.

2. "Don't ponder others."

3. Ponder the email from your grandmother in which she wrote, "I have been working on Spring cleaning and doing a good job. Went to the closet in the back bedroom to find my tennis shoes for the summer. And saw a plastic bag on the floor. Lo!!! It was the pics I have looked for for a few years, the ones from the box we used to keep in the dining rm and look at when you all came home. How strange."

4. Eat as many as fruits and vegetables as possible. Eat a cookie if you want.

5. Go out into the leaves.

6. Collect cartoons and other drawings from friends.

7. You may have been taken out on a sailboat on a very large lake more than once by someone kind, someone who liked you. Let your mind touch lightly upon the rocking motion and the sound of water lapping.

8. Iced berry tea, agave nectar. Some mint would be nice.

9. Consider a morning practice of Dragon's Breath—standing with legs slightly bent, slightly apart, then swinging the torso forward with a loud HA! You may want to do this twelve times

fast, until you are dizzy and laughing and stumbling around your bedroom.

10. Gratitude for subway drivers. (Engineers?) Especially that one who gave you that funny smile that time as he pulled away from 215th Street.

11. Collect piquant impressions, but don't be too acquisitive about it. Very few need actually be recorded.

12. Use words like "piquant" and "acquisitive." But use them sparingly.

> *I think it's time we stop,*
> *Children, what's that sound?*
> *Everybody look what's goin' down.*
>
> *You don't have to say you love me,*
> *just be close at hand.*

Dear Twentieth Century,

As a very small child in the Nixon years, even I was tired.

But there's ironic satisfaction to be found in Carole King's "It's Too Late" being number one the week you were born.

I wasn't your best citizen. I couldn't fix the business of the Panama Canal in my mind, try as I might, sitting in pigtails and watching the news.

And even though I knew about Ella Fitzgerald at a very young age, I thought her first name was "Ellafitz," last name "Gerald."

Dusty Springfield and Buffalo Springfield drifted unmoored for years, intermingling.

Roxy Music seemed important, but insidious.

It was all the disappearing sixties then, louche magic and hips.

All I mean to say is, I miss my can headphones. Car window handles. Decaying Chevy upholstery. The smell of warm grapes and peanuts at Pope and Airey's grocery store.

The world had heft and weight to it then.

We had Charlie Chaplin and Richard Pryor then.

I was born at the exhausted end of a barbarous century, but we had the good people.

The expected snow never came. You might say I'm only happy when I'm with you, or when I see a funny dog, or think about kittens or California or the South Seas and Pippi Longstocking. I woke up wondering if your forehead was made of diamonds and if you still hated me for hating Myth Busters. I let you make the coffee very strong. Then you stretched up and curled your arms around the air like a kung fu monk and walked out of the room. I can still hear you in there. You are expanding yourself and taking big breaths.

He stood and then quieted, and to my surprise did not leave again. I was expected to know which way was out and through and stepped on some acorn hats and helicopters, oak tags. (*What's an oak tag?*) We will be at our best here, outside the city. Hear that? That *hoo-hoo-hoo*? That's a turtledove, dove-colored, taupe-like and tapered, with sad, knowing eyes. Or a mourning dove maybe. I forget. And that's a maple. And that's…a tree with bright fuchsia blossoms. Crepe myrtle? India myrtle? India crepe myrtle. Something. And look below your feet at the macadam. I think that's macadam. The word sounds weird now. More black road, blue sky, green trees. That's all there is from here on out. Wait until we get to the barn. You can set up your typewriter on an old crate and scratch your beard and look picturesque. Look how faded and vintage-y everything looks around here. That huge old steering wheel. Your Levi's. The way our hands look together on our old quilt in the hayloft. Don't give me that look. You'll love it here. I'm going out to pick some wildflowers. When I get back, I'd like you to be handling those old bridles and things. Scratch your beard. Turn to me with that sad-eyed half-smile I like so much.

Sometimes you can help someone else through by plucking the air around them until they feel revived. The final step, though, is yours alone. You may discover that no one appreciates the grace of a skateboarder quite like you do. That your secret desire is to appear in a poster in the subway wearing green sequined underwear and *own* it. We all need time alone before returning to the marketplace with words and gestures that others mirror back to us. Some need more time than others, which is both blessing and curse. Think Spiderman. Think Witch of Blackbird Pond. *Most things happen at dusk.* Sometimes the trees will call you up a hill, particles slowing then turning counter-clockwise. One. Two. Three. When you let the drawing happen, that's your brand right there. A voice in your head like from a creepy '70s movie about kids who might be possessed or maybe were born that way. Literal woods. Literal dusk.

About the Author

JOANNA PENN COOPER is the author of the chapbooks *Mesmer* (dancing girl press) and *Crown* (forthcoming from Ravenna Press). Joanna's poems and prose have appeared in a number of journals, including *Poetry International*, *South Dakota Review*, *Opium*, *Supermachine*, *elimae*, and *Boog City*. Joanna earned a Ph.D. in American literature from Temple University and an MFA in poetry from New England College, and she has held full-time visiting positions at Marquette University and Fordham University. Joanna lives and writes in Brooklyn and keeps a blog at joannapenncooper.blogspot.com.

www.ingramcontent.com/pod-product-compliance
Lightning Source LLC
Chambersburg PA
CBHW060506080526
44584CB00015B/1577